Spaniels, Retrievers, and Other

SPORTING DOGS

by Tammy Gagne

CAPSTONE PRESS
a capstone imprint

Edge Books are published by Capstone Press,
1710 Roe Crest Drive, North Mankato, Minnesota 56003
www.mycapstone.com

Library of Congress Cataloging-in-Publication Data
Names: Gagne, Tammy, author.
Title: Spaniels, retrievers, and other sporting dogs / by Tammy Gagne.
Description: North Mankato, Minnesota : Capstone Press, [2017] | Series: Dog
    encyclopedias | Audience: Ages 9-12. | Audience: Grades 4 to 6. | Includes
    bibliographical references and index. | Description based on print version
    record and CIP data provided by publisher; resource not viewed.
Summary: Informative text and vivid photos introduce readers to various
    sporting dog breeds.
Identifiers: LCCN 2015046141 (print) | LCCN 2015043105 (ebook) |
    ISBN 978-1-5157-0305-1 (library binding) | ISBN 978-1-5157-0314-3
    (ebook pdf)
Subjects: LCSH: Hunting dogs—Juvenile literature. | Dog breeds—Juvenile
    literature.
Classification: LCC SF428.5 (print) | LCC SF428.5 .G34 2017 (ebook) |
    DDC 636.752—dc23
LC record available at http://lccn.loc.gov/2015046141

Editorial Credits
Alesha Halvorson, editor; Terri Poburka, designer; Kelly Garvin, media researcher;
Katy LaVigne, production specialist

Photo Credits
Newscom/Dorling Kindersley Universal Images Group, 23 (bottom); Shutterstock: Alex
White, 12 (top), Andreas Gradin, 14 (b), 20 (b), artcphotos, cover (top right), 7 (t), Barna
Tanko, 24 (t), Burry van den Brink, 15 (t), c.byatt-norman, 19 (t), Csanad Kiss, 24 (b),
CyberKat, 6 (t), cynoclub, 6 (b), 27 (b), 29 (b), DragoNika, 17 (t), Eric Isselee, backcover, 8 (b),
9 (b), 11 (b), 15 (b), 19 (b), Erik Lam, 7 (b), 12 (b), 13 (b), 29 (b), Iakov Filimonov, 18 (b), Irina
oxilixo Danilova, 16 (b), Ivonne Wierink, 17 (b), Jagodka, 10 (b), 26 (b), Jody., 26 (t), Joop
Snijder, cover (bottom right), juliazara, 4-5, Justin Black, 22 (t), Kirk Geisler, 1, Lenkadan,
8 (t), 9 (t), Linn Currie, 16 (t), 21 (t), Lorenzo Patoia, 11 (t), Mikkel Bigandt, 25 (t), Nejron
Photo, 25 (b), nicolasdecorte, 27 (t), Orientgold, 18 (t), otsphoto, 10 (t), Phil Stev, 14 (t),
Quayside, 22 (b), rebeccaashworth, 23 (t), Robynrg, cover (left), SikorskiFotografie, 28 (b),
StockPhotosLV, 13 (t), V.Belov, 20 (t), WilleeCole Photography, 21 (b)

Printed and bound in the United States of America.
009676F16

Table of Contents

Well-Rounded Companions

The American Kennel Club's (AKC) sporting group is made up of 30 dog breeds. Dogs in the sporting group are naturally active and alert. Each breed in this group was developed to work as a hunting dog. They accomplish this task in different ways, however. **Setters** and **pointers** help hunters by locating prey, such as birds. Spaniels chase the birds, forcing them into the air where hunters can see them. Retrievers help their owners by carrying the fallen birds to the hunter once the hunt is complete.

Sporting group dogs are popular pets, especially with active families. Whether these dogs hunt with their owners or hunt alone, they enjoy outdoor activities. Some are impressively fast runners. Others are known for their speed in the water. Some can both run fast and swim well.

Sporting group members that live as companion animals need regular exercise. Many enjoy feeling like they have a purpose. These breeds often excel at organized activities and dog sports, such as **agility** or rally training. Although these dogs share common traits, each one has something unique to offer. Get ready for a close look at each breed!

FUN FACT

The AKC is more than a dog registry. The AKC also educates the public about responsible dog ownership.

Brittany

Appearance:

Height: 17 to 21 inches (43 to 53 centimeters)
Weight: 30 to 40 pounds (14 to 18 kilograms)

The Brittany has a short, feathered coat. Most dogs of this breed are orange and white or liver and white. Liver is dark red-brown. Some dogs have patches of color. Others have roan coats, which means they have light-colored hairs mixed throughout their coats.

Personality: Brittanys love people, especially kids. This bird-dog has a strong hunting **instinct**. The Brittany is a poor match for a home with parakeets or other birds for this reason.

Breed Background: This breed used to be called the Brittany Spaniel. The AKC dropped the word "spaniel" from the dog's name in 1982. While the Brittany looks like a spaniel, it hunts like a pointer.

Country of Origin: France

Recognized by AKC: 1934

Training Notes: This smart breed loves pleasing its owner, so training a Brittany can be easy. These dogs respond well to positive and encouraging training methods. Brittanys also excel at competing in dog shows, agility events, and hunting tests.

Care Notes: This active breed needs a lot of exercise. Brittanys do well in homes with a large, fenced yard. These short-coated dogs require weekly brushing.

FUN FACT

A Brittany can smell a group of birds from 75 yards (69 meters) away!

Chesapeake Bay Retriever

Appearance:

Height: 21 to 26 inches (53 to 66 cm)
Weight: 55 to 80 pounds (25 to 36 kg)

The Chesapeake Bay Retriever has a double coat. The oily outer layer repels water. Even after a bath or swim, this breed can dry itself off just by shaking. Many Chessies are brown. The breed also comes in a red color, called sedge, and a tan color, called deadgrass.

Personality: Chessies are loyal to their human family members. This breed takes time to warm up to strangers and other animals though.

Country of Origin: United States

Recognized by AKC: 1878

Training Notes: Consistent training is a must for this breed. If left untrained these dogs can become bossy with their owners. Early **socialization** with other animals and with people is important for Chessies.

Care Notes: Chessies need a great deal of exercise. These athletic dogs prefer swimming and games of fetch as opposed to going for walks. Although this breed's coat is short, an owner must brush a Chessie's coat weekly to keep it looking its best.

FUN FACT

The Chesapeake Bay Retriever is the state dog of Maryland.

FAMOUS DOGS

General George Custer's Chesapeake Bay Retrievers joined him on the battlefield. Decades later President Theodore Roosevelt owned a Chessie named Sailor Boy. This dog was said to have come from the same family line as Custer's Chessies.

7

Clumber Spaniel

Appearance:
Height: 17 to 20 inches (43 to 51 cm)
Weight: 55 to 85 pounds (25 to 39 kg)

The Clumber Spaniel is the largest spaniel breed. When a Clumber pup is born, its coat is all white. Over time the dog develops either orange or lemon markings. Its thick, fluffy coat remains mostly white even as an adult, however.

Personality: Clumber Spaniels are usually quiet pets. Their personalities can range from friendly to **aloof**. People who want an outgoing dog should spend time with a whole litter. The puppy that greets you first is often the friendliest.

Country of Origin: France

Recognized by AKC: 1884

Training Notes: Clumber Spaniels need basic **obedience** training. These large dogs can be mischievous. Even a trained Clumber Spaniel will steal food from a countertop if the opportunity arises.

Care Notes: Owning this heavy-coated breed means lots of grooming. Clumber Spaniels are known for loud snoring and drooling. Many owners keep towels nearby. Clumber Spaniels also enjoy daily walks with their owners.

FUN FACT

The Clumber Spaniel is a rare breed. The AKC registers only about 200 Clumber Spaniel puppies each year.

Cocker Spaniel

Appearance:

Height: 14 to 15 inches (36 to 38 cm)
Weight: 20 to 35 pounds (9 to 16 kg)

When many people think of Cocker Spaniels, they imagine dogs with light tan or blond coats. But this sporty breed comes in many other colors, including black, brown, red, and silver. Some Cocker Spaniels are even particolored. This means they are a mixture of two or more colors.

Personality: This loyal, loving breed is filled with enthusiasm. When a Cocker Spaniel greets its favorite people, the dog doesn't just wag its tail. It usually wags its whole backside.

Breed Background: The Cocker Spaniel breed dates back to the 1300s in Spain.

Countries of Origin: Spain, England

Recognized by AKC: 1878

Training Notes: This intelligent breed is easily trained. Many Cocker Spaniels compete in organized activities, such as agility and obedience.

Care Notes: The Cocker Spaniel's long, floppy ears are a trademark of this breed. Those feathered ears and long coats require a great deal of grooming. Without regular brushing, the hair tangles quickly. Cocker Spaniels also need daily exercise, such as a long walk.

FUN FACT

Many years ago Cocker Spaniels and Springer Spaniels were born in the same litters. The smaller dogs were Cocker Spaniels, while the larger ones were Springer Spaniels.

FAMOUS DOGS

President Richard Nixon owned a Cocker Spaniel named Checkers.

Curly-Coated Retriever

Appearance:

Height: 23 to 27 inches (58 to 69 cm)

Weight: 65 to 100 pounds (29 to 45 kg)

The Curly-Coated Retriever has dense curls that can be either black or red-brown. The curls on the dog's floppy ears are usually looser than the ones on its body.

Personality: Curly-Coated Retrievers can seem shy at first. They love their human family members and want to please them. They take time to warm up to new people.

Country of Origin: United Kingdom

Recognized by AKC: 1924

Training Notes: This smart breed needs ongoing training because it tends to get bored easily. Slow to mature, the Curly-Coated Retriever often acts like a puppy for several years. It's a good idea to get this dog socialized right away too.

Care Notes: A Curly-Coated Retriever needs about an hour of exercise each day. Owners should make sure this time is filled with fun activities. These intelligent dogs are especially good at swimming. This breed needs to be brushed and bathed occasionally.

English Cocker Spaniel

Appearance:

Height: 15 to 17 inches (38 to 43 cm)
Weight: 26 to 34 pounds (12 to 15 kg)

Some people say that the English Cocker Spaniel has a "melting expression" with soft, dark eyes. Its silky coat can be solid black, red-brown, or various shades of red.

Personality: The English Cocker shares many traits with its American cousin, the Cocker Spaniel. Both breeds make pleasant pets. English Cocker Spaniels spend more time working as hunting dogs than American Cocker Spaniels do.

Breed Background: At one time the English Cocker Spaniel and the Cocker Spaniel were part of the same breed. The AKC separated these dogs into two breeds in 1946.

Country of Origin: England

Recognized by AKC: 1945

Training Notes: This intelligent breed learns quickly. Gentle, positive training works best with English Cocker Spaniels. They respond well to praise.

Care Notes: English Cocker Spaniels love to play. A couple sessions of fetch each day are enough of a workout for this breed. These dogs also need to be brushed and **stripped** regularly.

FUN FACT

Cocker Spaniels and English Cocker Spaniels are named after birds called woodcocks. These birds are the most common animals the breeds hunt.

English Setter

Appearance:
Height: 23 to 27 inches (58 to 69 cm)
Weight: 45 to 80 pounds (20 to 36 kg)

The English Setter has a long, flowing coat. Its coat comes in several colors, such as blue, lemon, and orange. Its speckled appearance is often referred to as belton, meaning "blended" or "flecked."

Personality: English Setters make excellent pets for families with older kids. They tend to shy away from younger children who play too roughly, however. This playful breed can act downright goofy.

Country of Origin: England

Recognized by AKC: 1884

Training Notes: This breed can be stubborn during training. Persistence pays off with this smart breed. Basic obedience training should begin at a young age with English Setters.

Care Notes: These dogs have a lot of energy. They require daily exercise, such as running in a fenced area. The English Setter's long, feathered coat must be brushed every other day to keep it looking its best.

FUN FACT

Setters are named for the crouched pose—or set—they take on when hunting game.

FAMOUS DOGS

President Herbert Hoover owned an English Setter named Eaglehurst Gillette.

English Springer Spaniel

Appearance:

Height: 19 to 20 inches (48 to 51 cm)
Weight: 40 to 50 pounds (18 to 23 kg)

English Springer Spaniels have varying coat patterns and hair lengths. Common colors for this breed include black and white, dark red-brown and white, and red and white. These graceful dogs also have long, lush ears.

Personality: All Springers love to play and spend time with their human family members. These dogs are known for their affectionate personalities. English Springer Spaniels also have a lot of energy and a big hunting drive.

Breed Background: Springer Spaniels were bred to act like several hunting dogs in one. They can point and retrieve game.

Country of Origin: England

Recognized by AKC: 1910

Training Notes: Some English Springer Spaniels have a natural hunting ability. Still, these dogs must be trained to perform this activity. Without positive training, Springers can become obnoxious and pushy.

Care Notes: To prevent **mats**, Springers should be brushed weekly. This breed needs regular exercise and loves to swim and play fetch.

FUN FACT

The Springer Spaniel is the fastest of all the spaniel breeds.

Flat-Coated Retriever

Appearance:

Height: 22 to 24 inches (56 to 61 cm)
Weight: 55 to 70 pounds (25 to 32 kg)

Many people mistake the Flat-Coated Retriever for a mixed breed. But this dog is a **purebred**. Its dark, flat coat gives the breed its name. Its coat can be either black or dark red-brown.

Personality: Flat-Coated Retrievers are friendly dogs that make great pets. People looking for a guard dog won't find it here. Flatties just want to have fun. The breed's nickname is the Peter Pan of dogs.

Breed Background: The Flat-Coated Retriever's ancestors include the Newfoundland and the Labrador Retriever.

Country of Origin: United Kingdom

Recognized by AKC: 1909

Training Notes: These playful dogs can take more time to train than other breeds. Flat-Coated Retrievers need both physical and mental **stimulation**.

Care Notes: Flat-Coated Retrievers need a lot of exercise. If owners do not provide an outlet for all its energy, this dog is likely to develop some behavior problems. Regular brushing and bathing are needed to keep this breed looking its best.

FUN FACT

Some Flat-Coated Retrievers work for the police as drug-sniffing dogs.

German Shorthaired Pointer

Appearance:

Height: 21 to 25 inches (53 to 64 cm)
Weight: 45 to 70 pounds (20 to 32 kg)

The German Shorthaired Pointer has a short, flat coat that resists water. This dog comes in several colors. Liver is among the most common.

Personality: This smart and loyal dog is an excellent pet for active families. Some people say German Shorthaired Pointers are excellent watchdogs too.

Breed Background: German Shorthaired Pointers are named for the pointing position they assume when hunting. With their eyes looking straight ahead, they raise their tail and one paw. Many people say a pointer looks like an arrow in this pose.

Country of Origin: Germany

Recognized by AKC: 1930

Training Notes: This breed's high energy can be an advantage for training. These active animals enjoy learning new things. Consistency and repetition are key for good training results.

Care Notes: German Shorthaired Pointers are incredibly athletic and need a lot of exercise. Their love of the water makes them ideal competitors in dock jumping. This popular canine sport involves chasing a ball that is thrown into water. Occasional brushing is important too.

FUN FACT

A German Shorthaired Pointer's nose is always the same color as its coat.

Golden Retriever

Appearance:
Height: 21 to 24 inches (53 to 61 cm)
Weight: 55 to 75 pounds (25 to 34 kg)

The Golden Retriever is one of the most popular sporting breeds. Named for its color, this dog has a double coat that ranges from light to dark gold. Its coat can be wavy or straight.

Personality: These friendly dogs are known for their obedience and devotion. Goldens want nothing more than to please their owners.

Country of Origin: United Kingdom

Recognized by AKC: 1925

Training Notes: This intelligent breed is among the easiest dogs to train. Basic obedience training may also strengthen the bond between a Golden Retriever and its human family members.

Care Notes: Providing this breed with daily exercise is important in order to maintain physical and mental fitness. A Golden Retriever's water-repellent double coat needs regular brushing and bathing.

FUN FACT
A Golden Retriever always has a lighter coat as a puppy. The color of a pup's ears is the best sign of what its adult color will be.

FAMOUS DOGS
The canine stars of the *Air Bud* movies are Golden Retrievers.

Gordon Setter

Appearance:

Height: 23 to 27 inches (58 to 69 cm)
Weight: 45 to 75 pounds (20 to 34 kg)

The Gordon Setter has a black and tan coat with a long, feathered tail. The silky hair may be straight or slightly wavy. Dog enthusiasts are especially fond of this breed's tan eyebrows.

Personality: Gordon Setters are playful puppies. They keep this trait throughout adulthood. They make excellent pets for people who can give them plenty of space. This is not a good breed for city living.

Breed Background: The Gordon Setter got its name from Duke Alexander Gordon, who owned members of the breed. Before this time, the dog was known as the Black and Tan Setter.

Country of Origin: Scotland

Recognized by AKC: 1884

Training Notes: Gordon Setters are highly intelligent, so training these dogs can be easy. Positive methods of training are necessary for this breed. Gordon Setters also have incredible memories. Gordon Setters used for hunting can remember places where they found birds for up to one year.

Care Notes: Gordon Setters need daily exercise on a leash or in a fenced area. Weekly brushing is important to keep its silky coat mat-free.

FUN FACT

The Gordon Setter is the largest of all setter breeds.

Irish Setter

Appearance:

Height: 25 to 27 inches (64 to 69 cm)
Weight: 60 to 70 pounds (27 to 32 kg)

The Irish Setter is known for its soft, deep-red coat. The hair on its head and feet is short. It has longer hair on its ears and the rest of its body.

Personality: This affectionate breed is active and playful. These dogs need an active family. They also tend to bark often.

Country of Origin: Unknown; believed to be Ireland

Recognized by AKC: 1878

Training Notes: Irish Setters are smart dogs with a strong hunting instinct. Once these dogs are trained to hunt birds, they never forget the skill. Short, positive training sessions work best for Irish Setters because their lively personality keeps them constantly on the go.

Care Notes: These athletic dogs need room to run, such as in a fenced area, or they need to be taken on long walks daily. Grooming an Irish Setter requires regular brushing to prevent its hair from tangling.

FUN FACT

Irish Setters weren't always red. The first members of this breed were mostly white with a few red patches. Dogs with this coloring are now known as Red and White Setters.

FAMOUS DOGS

President Harry Truman owned an Irish Setter named Mike.

Labrador Retriever

Appearance:
Height: 21 to 24 inches (53 to 61 cm)
Weight: 55 to 80 pounds (25 to 36 kg)

The Labrador Retriever comes in three colors: black, chocolate, and yellow. The layered coat is slightly oily. It helps keep the animal warm and afloat when retrieving game in the water. The coat also resists water, so it dries quickly.

Personality: This popular pet is among the friendliest dog breeds. Labs love people of all ages. They make great pets for active families who enjoy the outdoors.

Breed Background: The Labrador Retriever was developed in Newfoundland. This breed was named after the nearby Labrador Sea.

Country of Origin: Canada

Recognized by AKC: 1917

Training Notes: These smart animals can be trained for a variety of sports and other tasks. Labs are often the top dogs in obedience competitions. They are also trained to work as therapy dogs and police dogs. Positive obedience training is essential for Labs.

Care Notes: This active breed needs a lot of exercise. Labs love to run and swim. A Lab's coat must be brushed and bathed occasionally to keep it looking its best.

FUN FACT
Labrador Retrievers have been known to jump distances up to 27 feet (8 m) when retrieving from water.

FAMOUS DOGS
The title character from the *Marley & Me* books and film is a Lab.

Nova Scotia Duck Tolling Retriever

FUN FACT

The Nova Scotia Duck Tolling Retriever was first known as the "Little River Duck Dog."

Appearance:
Height: 17 to 21 inches (43 to 53 cm)
Weight: 35 to 50 pounds (16 to 23 kg)

The Nova Scotia Duck Tolling Retriever is a red-orange dog with white on its face, chest, and feet. Many dog enthusiasts say the red color makes this dog look like a fox.

Personality: The smallest of retriever breeds, Nova Scotia Duck Tolling Retrievers are pleasant and happy dogs. This dog can become too independent without a purpose, though. Tollers do best with hunters or active families.

Breed Background: This retriever was named for its hunting style. The dog lures ducks to the hunter, going back and forth between **baiting** and hiding.

Country of Origin: Canada

Recognized by AKC: 2003

Training Notes: This breed learns quickly and easily. Owners must make training fun. If a Toller becomes bored, it may develop stubbornness. Calm and positive training methods work best for these dogs.

Care Notes: A Nova Scotia Duck Tolling Retriever needs about an hour of exercise each day. As long as it gets its workout, a Toller can live in either the city or the country. Regular grooming and brushing, such as weekly or every other week, are necessary for this dog's medium-length coat.

Pointer

Appearance:

Height: 23 to 28 inches (58 to 71 cm)
Weight: 45 to 75 pounds (20 to 34 kg)

A Pointer's muscular body is covered with short hair. Its coat comes in a variety of colors and markings. Among the most common is white with black, lemon, or dark red-brown markings.

Personality: Pointers are loyal dogs that make great family pets. This breed always wants to be part of the fun. If its human family is outdoors, a Pointer wants to be outside as well.

Breed Background: The oldest of all sporting dogs, Pointers have been working alongside hunters since the 1600s.

Country of Origin: England

Recognized by AKC: 1884

Training Notes: Pointers are challenging to train. Owners who make ongoing training a part of their routine usually have the best results with Pointers. Early socialization and basic obedience training will help with this breed's high energy level too.

Care Notes: Like many other sporting breeds, Pointers are active dogs. The ideal owner has a fenced yard or takes this dog for long walks on a daily basis. Pointers require occasional bathing and brushing.

FUN FACT

The Westminster Kennel Club's logo features a Pointer named Sensation.

Spinone Italiano

Appearance:
Height: 22 to 27 inches (56 to 69 cm)
Weight: 62 to 82 pounds (28 to 37 kg)

The Spinone Italiano is best known for the shaggy fur all over its face. This dog has hairy eyebrows as well as a long beard and mustache. The Spinone may be orange and white, brown and white, or all white.

Personality: This active breed loves spending time with people. Owners who take these dogs along for hikes will return home with happy pets. Friendly and good-natured, most Spinoni are not **aggressive**.

Country of Origin: Italy

Recognized by AKC: 2000

Training Notes: This smart dog is easy to train. Some members of the breed can be stubborn. Spinoni owners should begin socializing this breed early.

Care Notes: Owners may want to keep a towel handy with this breed. Many people refer to this dog's slobber as "Spinone slime." These dogs also love to be active, so daily exercise is important. Their medium-length hair should be combed every other week.

FUN FACT

The Spinone Italiano is one of the calmest retriever breeds.

Sussex Spaniel

Appearance:

Height: 13 to 15 inches (33 to 38 cm)
Weight: 35 to 45 pounds (16 to 20 kg)

With its long body and short legs, the Sussex Spaniel looks like a small Cocker Spaniel. The breed is also known for its golden-liver color. It has a feathery coat with wavy ears and big, hazel eyes.

Personality: Sussex Spaniels offer owners the best of both worlds when it comes to personality. At home these dogs make calm and well-mannered pets. Outside, however, they transform into much more active animals.

Country of Origin: England

Recognized by AKC: 1884

Training Notes: Sussex Spaniels are fast learners. Still, some can take time to obey commands. Owners should be patient when training Sussex Spaniels and always use heartfelt praise.

Care Notes: Owners should take their Sussex Spaniels for long walks or hikes regularly. This breed also appreciates the company of other dogs. Its soft coat should be brushed weekly.

FUN FACT

The Sussex Spaniel was named after Sussex, England, where the breed was developed.

Vizsla

Appearance:
Height: 21 to 24 inches (53 to 61 cm)
Weight: 48 to 66 pounds (22 to 30 kg)

The short-coated Vizsla (*VEESH-lah*) is a golden, rust-brown color. Its hair, eyes, nose, and nails are all this color too.

FUN FACT

The Vizsla makes a great pet for owners with sensitive noses. This clean breed has virtually no odor at all.

Personality: A Vizsla's two favorite things are attention and exercise. Owners who give this breed plenty of both get a wonderful companion in return. After a good play session, most Vizslas can be found relaxing at their owners' feet.

Country of Origin: Hungary

Recognized by AKC: 1960

Training Notes: Vizslas are smart yet **quirky** dogs. Vizslas are designed to hunt, but owners must be persistent when training this breed. Positive techniques, such as praise and food awards, work best with Vizslas.

Care Notes: Vizslas need about two hours of intense activity every day. These dogs must run to burn up all their energy. Their short coats should be bathed and brushed weekly.

Weimaraner

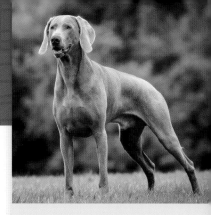

Appearance:
Height: 23 to 27 inches (58 to 69 cm)
Weight: 55 to 85 pounds (25 to 39 kg)

Weimaraners are known for their muscular bodies and unusual color. These dogs are a unique silvery gray. The breed is nicknamed the "Gray Ghost."

FUN FACT
All Weimaraner puppies are born with blue eyes. They turn yellow as the dogs get older.

Personality: Weimaraners make excellent family pets. However they tend to bark a lot. Sometimes they do this to announce a visitor. Other times they simply enjoy making noise.

Breed Background:
The Weimaraner breed was developed in the early 1800s as a hunting dog in Germany.

Country of Origin: Germany

Recognized by AKC: 1943

Training Notes: This breed is intelligent yet independent. Most times a Weimaraner is easy to train. Puppy obedience classes should begin right away.

Care Notes: Weimaraners are speedy runners and need lots of exercise every day. This short-haired breed is easy to groom and only needs a bath every few weeks.

Welsh Springer Spaniel

Appearance:
Height: 17 to 19 inches (43 to 48 cm)
Weight: 35 to 55 pounds (16 to 25 kg)

The Welsh Springer Spaniel has a red and white feathered coat. The hair is naturally straight and lies flat against the dog's body. Its coat is considered waterproof and **weatherproof**.

Personality: Welsh Springers love their human family members. They love children who treat them respectfully. Welsh Springers can be slow to accept strangers.

Country of Origin: Wales

Recognized by AKC: 1906

Training Notes: These dogs train easily, but early socialization is important. Welsh Springers that aren't exposed to people as puppies can become shy as adult dogs.

Care Notes: This athletic dog needs daily exercise or walks. Regular brushing is important for Welsh Springers. These dogs also need their ears cleaned often. Like other spaniel breeds, Welsh Springers are prone to ear infections.

Wirehaired Pointing Griffon

Appearance:

Height: 20 to 24 inches (51 to 61 cm)
Weight: 50 to 60 pounds (23 to 27 kg)

The Wirehaired Pointing Griffon has a thick, double coat. The medium-length hair comes in a variety of colors. Brown and gray dogs are the most popular members of this rare breed.

Personality: Wirehaired Pointing Griffons enjoy entertaining their families. These fun-loving dogs thrive when participating in outdoor activities.

Breed Background: This breed was developed by crossing a German Griffon with a French Pointer. Today's Griffons also have retrievers, setters, and spaniels in their ancestry.

Country of Origin: Netherlands

Recognized by AKC: 1887

Training Notes: This breed is intelligent and easy to train. Griffons are fast learners and want to please their owners.

Care Notes: Wirehaired Pointing Griffon owners should know that this breed loves the water. Whenever this dog is near a pool or lake, it will likely jump in. This highly active breed needs a lot of exercise. Regular brushing will keep a Griffon's wiry coat looking neat.

FUN FACT

The Wirehaired Pointing Griffon's nickname is the "Supreme Gun Dog" because of its hunting ability.

American Water Spaniel

Known for: retrieving waterfowl
Country of Origin: United States
Recognized by AKC: 1940

....

Boykin Spaniel

Known for: retrieving from both land and water
Country of Origin: United States
Recognized by AKC: 2009

....

Field Spaniel

Known for: dedication as a hunter
Country of Origin: England
Recognized by AKC: 1894

....

German Wirehaired Pointer ▶

Known for: ability to hunt
  in harsh conditions
Country of Origin: Germany
Recognized by AKC: 1959

....

Irish Red and White Setter

Known for: being the older of the two
  Irish Setter breeds
Country of Origin: Ireland
Recognized by AKC: 2009

....

Irish Water Spaniel

Known for: talent as a guard dog
Country of Origin: Ireland
Recognized by AKC: 1884

....

Lagotto Romagnolo ▶

Known for: curly coat
Country of Origin: Italy
Recognized by AKC: 2001

....

Wirehaired Vizsla ▶

Known for: heavy build and wiry coat
Country of Origin: Hungary
Recognized by AKC: 2014

....

Glossary

aggressive (uh-GREH-siv)—strong and forceful

agility (uh-GI-luh-tee)—the ability to move fast and easily

aloof (uh-LOOF)—distant or not friendly

bait (BAYT)—to annoy or taunt

instinct (IN-stingkt)—behavior that is natural rather than learned

mat (MAT)—a thick, tangled mass of hair

obedience (oh-BEE-dee-uhns)—obeying rules and commands

pointer (POIN-ter)—a type of dog breed used for hunting, flushing, and retrieving game; its name derives from the dog's instinct to point at game

purebred (PYOOR-bred)—having ancestors of the same breed or kind of animal

quirky (KWUR-kee)—having a peculiar trait or a strange way of acting

setter (SET-er)—one of several breeds of hunting dogs that are trained to stand stiffly and point the muzzle toward the scented game

socialize (SOH-shuh-lize)—to train to get along with people and other dogs

stimulate (STIM-yuh-late)—to encourage interest or activity in a person or animal

strip (STRIP)—to remove dead hair

weatherproof (WETH-uhr-proof)—able to withstand exposure to all kinds of weather

Read More

Bowman, Chris. *Golden Retrievers*. Awesome Dogs. Minneapolis, Minn.: Bellweather Media, 2015.

Gagne, Tammy. *Spaniels: Loyal Hunting Companions*. Hunting Dogs. North Mankato, Minn.: Capstone Press, 2013.

Mattern, Joanne. *Irish Red and White Setters*. Dogs. Edina, Minn.: ABDO Pub. Co., 2012.

Internet Sites

FactHound offers a safe, fun way to find Internet sites related to this book. All of the sites on FactHound have been researched by our staff.

Here's all you do:

Visit *www.facthound.com*

Type in this code: 9781515703051

Check out projects, games and lots more at
www.capstonekids.com

Index